Feeling Angry

For a free color catalog describing Gareth Stevens' list of high-quality books and multimedia programs, call 1-800-542-2595 (USA) or 1-800-461-9120 (Canada). Gareth Stevens Publishing's Fax: (414) 225-0377.
See our catalog, too, on the World Wide Web: http://gsinc.com

The author and original publisher would like to thank the staff and pupils of the following schools for their help in the making of this book: St. Barnabas Church of England Primary School, Pimlico; Mayfield Primary School, Cambridge; St. Peter's Church of England Primary School, Sible Hedingham.

Library of Congress Cataloging-in-Publication Data

Althea.
     Feeling angry / by Althea Braithwaite; photographs by Charlie Best; illustrations by Conny Jude.
        p. cm. — (Exploring emotions)
     Includes bibliographical references and index.
     Summary: Examines the nature, causes, and effects of anger and discusses how to deal with it.
     ISBN 0-8368-2116-5 (lib. bdg.)
     1. Anger in children—Juvenile literature. [1. Anger.] I. Best, Charlie, ill. II. Jude, Conny, ill. III. Title. IV. Series: Althea. Exploring emotions.
BF723.A4A48   1998
152.4'7—dc21   98-10295

This North American edition first published in 1998 by
Gareth Stevens Publishing
1555 North RiverCenter Drive, Suite 201
Milwaukee, Wisconsin 53212 USA

This U.S. edition © 1998 by Gareth Stevens, Inc.
First published in 1997 by A & C Black (Publishers) Limited, 35 Bedford Row, London WC1R 4JH. Text © 1997 by Althea Braithwaite. Photographs © 1997 by Charlie Best. Illustrations © 1997 by Conny Jude. Additional end matter © 1998 by Gareth Stevens, Inc.

Series consultant: Dr. Dorothy Rowe

Gareth Stevens series editor: Dorothy L. Gibbs
Editorial assistant: Diane Laska

Printed in Mexico

1 2 3 4 5 6 7 8 9 02 01 00 99 98

Exploring Emotions

Feeling Angry

Althea

Photographs by
Charlie Best

Illustrations by
Conny Jude

Gareth Stevens Publishing
MILWAUKEE

What does it mean to be angry?

When you are irritable or grouchy, it might be because you aren't feeling very well, or because you have to do something you don't like to do.

Do I have to go to Aunt Jane's, Dad?

4

Mom's upset because my room is a mess.

People can be grouchy without getting angry and losing their tempers.

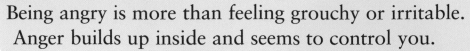

Being angry is more than feeling grouchy or irritable.
Anger builds up inside and seems to control you.

My voice gets harsh, and my skin feels tight.

My stomach feels all knotted up.

How do you feel when you're angry?

We sometimes get angry when we want something to turn out well, but it doesn't.

Richard says, "I get angry when I'm trying to build a model and it keeps falling apart."

What other things make us angry?

- When I know I'm wrong, or I feel guilty about something.

- When my older brother makes me feel like a fool in front of my friends.

- When I trip over a step, I get angry at the step.

Everyone gets angry at times, and, sometimes, a person needs to get angry.

When someone takes something of yours, or treats you unfairly, you have a right to be angry.

I get very angry when other people pick on me.

What makes you angry?

9

Sometimes it's easy to see when people are angry. You can tell just by looking at them. They might turn pale or get red in the face.

Do you know how you look when you're angry?

My friend clenches her fists, like this.

How do you act when you're angry?

Some people get very quiet or won't say anything. Other people have to let out their feelings.

I want to scream to get it out of my system.

I say things I don't mean.

Jacob says, "When I lose my temper, I lose control and lash out in all directions. I scare myself — and everyone else!"

Exploding with anger usually makes you and the people around you even more upset. Can you think of ways to let out your anger without hurting yourself or anyone else?

Sometimes it helps to be by yourself. Natalie says, "I stomp all the way up the stairs and slam my bedroom door. Everyone knows when I'm angry! Then I lie down on my bed and fall asleep — being angry makes me very tired."

13

People need time to calm down after they've been angry. Richard says, "Before I can say I'm sorry, I have to do something to make myself feel better. So, I play computer games or read a book."

We have to learn to deal with our anger. Talking about it helps sometimes.

When I go for a walk with Mom and Dad, they're too busy enjoying themselves to listen to me.

If you tell someone else what is making you angry, that person might be able to help or suggest a solution. If you're too angry to talk about it, wait until you calm down.

Holly remembers, "I was very angry with Grandpa for dying. He didn't say goodbye to me, and I wanted to tell him I loved him.

I told my friend Jasmine about it. While I was talking, I started to remember some of the fun things Grandpa and I had done together. Talking about it made me feel less angry and less sad. Remembering the good times became the most important thing."

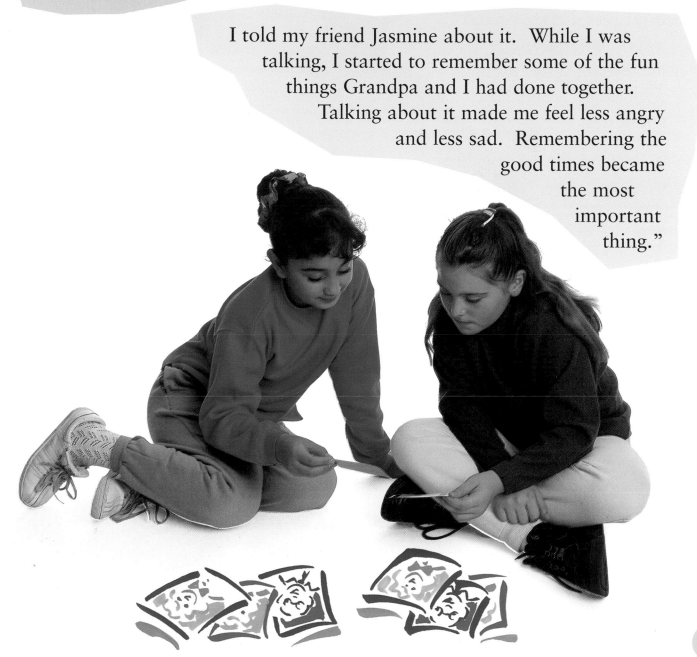

17

It often helps to talk to the person who's making you angry. If you can admit you are angry and explain why, it will help that person understand. It will make you feel better, too.

Of course, if you both are angry, talking might be difficult — or impossible.

Wait until you calm down before you say anything. Try not to shout or use angry words. If the other person is still angry, he or she might not listen carefully, and you might have to repeat what you said.

If you'll listen to me, I'll listen to you.

The other person might have good reasons for being angry, too. If you both are too angry to talk calmly, it's better to wait and talk later.

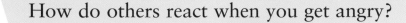

How do others react when you get angry?

Many people don't know how to cope with the anger of others. They feel frightened, and, then, they get angry, too.

I get into big trouble when I'm angry. No one ever asks why I'm upset.

I always
end up being sent
to my room!

Adults sometimes don't take time to find out why you're angry. Instead, they punish you for behaving badly. Being sent to your room will, at least, give you time to calm down and stop feeling angry.

When someone is angry with you, do you always know the reason? If you don't, you probably feel confused. The person might be angry because of something you did. If so, try to find out what it was. Then, say you're sorry and try to make amends.

I used to make everyone angry without knowing why! Now I've learned to stop bothering them with my chattering when they're trying to work.

When a person gets angry with you, it might be because someone else made him or her angry, or the person might be tired or upset about something else.

Sometimes, when Mom's very tired, she loses her temper and shouts at me — usually over nothing. Later, she says she's sorry.

When someone is angry with you, it doesn't mean the person doesn't like you, even though it might feel that way at the time.

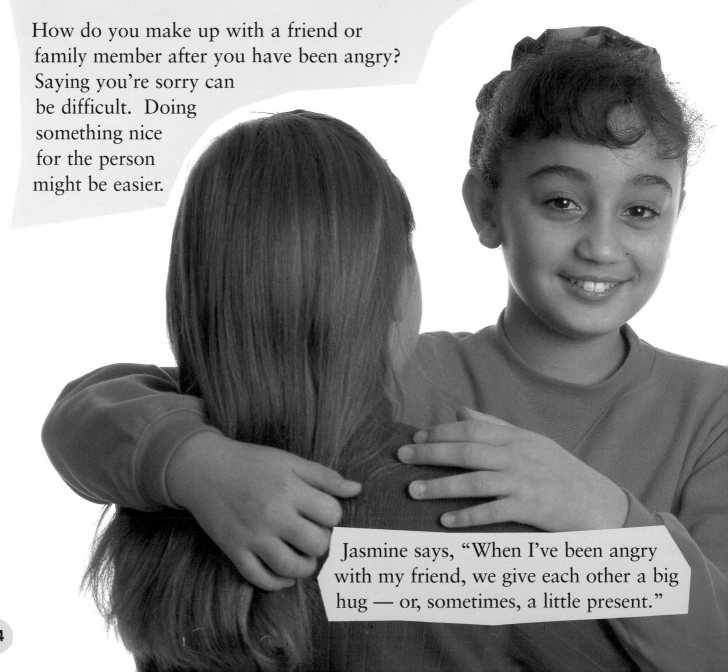

Try to forget the mean things people say to hurt you when they are angry. Afterward, they usually wish they hadn't said them.

How do you make up with a friend or family member after you have been angry? Saying you're sorry can be difficult. Doing something nice for the person might be easier.

Jasmine says, "When I've been angry with my friend, we give each other a big hug — or, sometimes, a little present."

We just say "friends?" Then everything is all right.

You might even find that you can laugh about it afterward. The important thing is to be friends again, and to show you care and are sorry. We have to be prepared to forgive other people and forget about our arguments. We should forgive ourselves, too, for getting angry in the first place.

For Teachers and Parents
A Note from Dorothy Rowe

Everyone gets angry at times and, sometimes, with good reason. Teachers and parents know that feeling angry is a common problem for children. Adults sometimes forget, however, that, in order to help, they first must find out how the child sees the problem.

A child won't see a situation the same way an adult does for the simple reason that no two people, whatever their ages, ever see things in exactly the same way. An adult shouldn't assume he or she knows what's wrong with a child but, rather, should explore possible reasons for the child's anger by seeking answers to questions like: "Does this child get angry when he or she is frightened?" or "Does this child handle anger the way he or she sees his or her parents handling it?"

Dozens of reasons are possible answers to the question, "Why does this child behave this way?" Thinking of these alternatives helps the adult ask better questions. The answers, however, can come only from the child.

Feeling angry isn't a problem that can be solved once and for all. It is a dilemma we face all our lives. We need to learn how to control our anger, even when it's justified, by finding ways to channel the anger. Adults must be prepared to share with children their own experiences, including the difficulties they have had dealing with anger. They should not pretend to provide easy solutions to controlling anger. This way, adults and children can explore the anger dilemma together.

Suggestions for Discussion

To start a discussion and get everyone involved, you and the children could write lists of all the things that make you angry. Then, compare lists. If you think individual lists would take too much time, you could, instead, have the children help you compile a single list of specific situations that often make people angry. Then, have them rate each situation in terms of whether it makes them feel "very angry" or just "annoyed" or whether they "don't mind" at all.

Some examples of situations that make people angry are:

- Embarrassing yourself or feeling you've made a fool of yourself in some way, like clumsily tripping over a step.

- Being wrongly accused of taking something without permission.

- Having someone borrow something of yours without asking.

Many of the reasons for anger and the ways to cope with it can be discussed with children while going through this book, page by page. The following points might help start your discussions.

Pages 6-7
Many other descriptions of how people feel when they are angry can be discovered and talked about.

Page 8
Some people hate feeling foolish, and they can get very angry when they feel that way. Others clown their way through mishaps and don't seem to mind them. We need to be able to laugh at ourselves, instead of getting angry, when we do something foolish or when we are being teased.

Page 9
Anger is an uncomfortable feeling that can cause both emotional and physical distress. Learning to control anger helps to avoid or reduce the distress. Controlling anger, however, does not mean ignoring or denying angry feelings. Not admitting you are angry, especially when you have a right to be, also can cause distress.

Page 11
Some people become so agitated when they are angry that they don't know what to do with themselves or how to act.

Page 12
Some children, especially small children, are prone to temper tantrums. They want life to be organized and under control and can become very frightened when everything seems to fall apart. They must learn ways to cope with these moments.

Page 13
Sometimes, something as simple as punching a cushion can help get rid of anger in a safe way. Children could write descriptions or paint pictures of how they get rid of angry feelings.

Pages 14-16
Children often can calm down by talking to a pet, or to one of their toys, about how they feel. Sometimes, just thinking about things we care about or enjoy doing will help us calm down.

Page 17
A whole area of anger that some people don't recognize, or don't want to address, is feeling angry when a loved one, or someone very close, dies. Many people think they shouldn't show this anger, and they try to repress it.

Pages 18-19
When they are angry, some people often help themselves by counting to 10, or to 100, and even back again, before trying to talk to the people with whom they are angry.

Pages 22-23
When someone is angry with you, it usually is better to be quiet at first. Wait until later, after the person has had a chance to calm down, before asking why he or she was angry.

Pages 24-25
Making up with people and forgiving each other is very important to resolving situations of anger. People communicate forgiveness in many different ways.

More Books to Read

Don't Rant and Rave on Wednesdays! The Children's Anger Control Book. Adolph Moser (Landmark Editions)

Emotional Ups and Downs. Good Health Guides (series). Enid Fisher (Gareth Stevens)

From Mad to Worse. Jim and Joan Boulden (Boulden Publishing)

Growing Up with Angry Feelings. Rona D. Schenkerman (Bureau for At-Risk Youth)

How I Learned to Control My Temper. Debbie Pincus (Center for Applied Psychology)

When You Get Really Mad! Sharon Landeen (Ol' Stone Press)

Videos to Watch

Anger: Rage and You. (Sunburst Communications)

Angry John. (Pyramid Film & Video)

How to Go from Mad to Glad. (Sunburst Communications)

Just Chill. (Sunburst Communications)

Web Sites to Visit

www.cts.com/crash/habtsmrt/text1.htm   members.aol.com/angriesout/

Due to the dynamic nature of the Internet, some web sites stay current longer than others. To find additional web sites, use a reliable search engine with one or more of the following keywords to help you locate information about feeling angry. Keywords: *anger, argue, behavior, conflict, emotions, feelings, temper.*

Glossary

amends — something said or done to try to make up for hurting another person or causing a loss.

anger — a strong feeling of unfriendliness, annoyance, irritation, or conflict.

annoy — to bother someone; to get on someone's nerves.

argument — a verbal, sometimes angry, disagreement; a quarrel.

behave — to act in a particular way that is considered correct or proper.

clench — to close up, grasp, or squeeze tightly.

cope — to deal with, or overcome, a problem or a difficult situation.

harsh — unpleasant, unfeeling, disapproving, cruel.

impossible — extremely difficult to deal with; not possible; not able to be accomplished.

irritable — easily annoyed or offended; bad-tempered.

lash — to strike at or attack suddenly, sometimes violently, especially with harsh words.

react — to act in a way that responds to the action or influence of an outside source.

revenge — something said or done to get back at, or get even with, another person who has caused hurt or loss.

solution — the answer to a problem; an explanation.

temper — a person's mood, state of mind, or way of feeling; an emotional outburst.

understand — to recognize, accept, and care about the circumstances of another person.

Index